THE THREE WOMEN OF ADVENT

*CONNECTING THE DOTS TO
THEIR LIFE, LEGACY AND LESSONS*

Gloria K. Ashby

The Three Women of Advent
Connecting the Dots to Their Life, Legacy, and Lessons
Gloria K. Ashby

To contact the author:
email: gloriaashby.connectingdots@gmail.com

Copyright © 2022 Gloria K. Ashby. All rights reserved. Except for brief quotations for review purposes, no part of this book may be reproduced in any form without prior written permission from the author.

ISBN (Print): 979-8-9861119-0-2
ISBN (E-book): 979-8-9861119-1-9

All scripture quotations, unless otherwise indicated, are taken from *The Holy Bible, New Revised Standard Version of the Bible.* Copyright ©1989 by the Division of Christian Education of the National Council of the Churches of Christ in the United States of America.

Scripture quotations taken from *The Message.* Copyright © 1993, 1994, 1995, 1996, 2000, 2001, 2002. Used by permission of NavPress Publishing Group. All rights reserved.

Scripture quotations taken from *The Holy Bible, New Living Translation.* Copyright © 1996, 2004 by Tyndale Charitable Trust. Used by permission of Tyndale House Publishers, Wheaton, Illinois 60189. All rights reserved.

Scripture quotations from *The Holy Bible, English Standard Version.* Copyright © 2001 by Crossway, a publishing ministry of Good News Publishers. All rights reserved.

 Scripture quotations from *The Holy Bible, New International Version.* Copyright ©1973, 1978, 1984 by International Bible Society. Used by permission of Zondervan Publishing House. All rights reserved.

For all the women who have undergirded my life
with love and leadership

and

to Methodist Women's Fellowship of
Prosper United Methodist Church,
women who are a constant source of
encouragement and abiding friendship.

Contents

	Acknowledgments	i
1	If It Were Not for the Women...	1
2	Elizabeth	11
3	Mary	23
4	Anna	35
5	A Closing Note	45
6	Notes	51
7	Sources	55
8	Meet the Author	57

Acknowledgements

No book comes together through a solo effort. Instead, a cloud of witnesses teams up and encircles an individual to inspire, encourage, and support the project. This one is no exception. I extend my heartfelt thanks to Diane Galloway, the friend who first encouraged me to turn my talk on the topic into this book; my friend Nan Vance who painstakingly applied her wisdom and experience to help edit the content; and to my husband, without whose support and patience, this study might still be in draft.

IF IT WERE NOT FOR THE WOMEN...

Women over the centuries pioneered many of our modern-day conveniences and breakthrough discoveries. For instance, did you know that if it were not for women, we would not have[1]:

—Technology for microwaves and X-rays, both of which Madame Marie Curie made possible with her discovery of radioactivity.

—Wireless WIFI, whose foundation evolved from secret communications language developed in World War II by an actor better known for her beauty, Hedy Lamar.

—A safe launch of man into space and Neil Armstrong to the moon without the mathematical genius of Katherine Johnson and Christine Darden.

—Our modern home security systems without Marie Van Brittan Brown, who invented and patented the first closed-circuit television security system after she became disgruntled by the slow response of police calls for help in her New York neighborhood.

—A myriad of inventions, such as the dishwasher, solar power heating system, Liquid Paper, Scotchgard, and Kevlar, that super strong fiber material used for bulletproof vests and the Ov-glove.

The list could go for pages. Women have achieved excellence in every field of society, though they often received little acclaim or recognition for it at the time. Historically, societal norms and governments tended to relegate women to matters of the home or behind-the-scenes. They were not perceived as key players.

The patriarchal society of Biblical times can also leave the casual reader with a similar misperception that women were too small to count. Yet, a closer look at Scripture reveals a vastly different picture. From the beginning of time, God created woman for a purpose. That purpose was to be a helper:

*God said, "It's not good
for the Man to be alone;
I'll make him a helper, a companion."...
The Man named the cattle,
named the birds of the air,
named the wild animals;
but he didn't find a suitable companion.*
Genesis 2:18 & 20; The Message

Neither the cattle, the birds of the air, nor any of the animals were suitable for what God had in mind as man's companion. He understood the deeper need, and it was for a helper.

WHAT DOES IT MEAN TO BE A HELPER ACCORDING TO GOD?

In today's conversations, we often misconstrue the word *helper* to define someone quite different than its intended meaning in Biblical times. To that point, the Miriam-Webster online dictionary defines *helper* as:[2]

---

*one that helps, especially
a relatively unskilled worker
who assists a skilled worker
usually by manual labor.*

Synonyms: *adjunct, adjutant, aid, aide, apprentice, assistant, coadjutor, deputy, helpmate, helpmeet, lieutenant, mate, sidekick.*

As the oldest of four and with a staunchly independent nature, I rebelled against that definition. And who can blame me? It implies someone who is weak, a lessor of two who can work only under supervision. The definition fails miserably to capture the true identity God gave woman when He created her.

The Hebrew term used in Genesis for *helper* is *ezer*. The Old Testament always and only used *ezer* in the context of vitally important and powerful acts of rescue and support. Likewise, it is the same term used throughout Psalms to describe the nature of God (for example, see Psalm 10:14; 30:10-11; 54:4; and 72:12-14) and Hebrews 13:6 in which the author declared,

---

So we can say with confidence,
"The Lord is my helper,
so I will have no fear.
What can mere people do to me?"
Hebrews 13:6; NLT

Women are called to live into God's very nature as a helper. And we can hardly call God a sidekick or an "unskilled worker who assists a skilled worker [mankind]."

According to Rabbi David Freedman, the word *ezer* is a combination of two roots: *-z-r*, meaning "to rescue, to save," and *g-z-r*, meaning "to be strong."[3] By applying these definitions, the inspired Word of God paints a very different portrait of the *ezer*-styled woman and the role God intended her to play in His unfolding story. Instead of the unskilled worker capable of only manual labor, she is strong enough to give the assistance necessary to rescue or save another.

The New Testament reflects this same sentiment of helper in *ezer's* Greek equivalent, *boetheia*.[4] A study of this word expands the picture of a helper even further. *Boetheia*, a feminine noun derived from *boēthéō* (Strong's 997), means a brand of help, especially critical assistance that meets an urgent situation, delivering very needed aid.[5]

Interestingly, *boetheia* is the same word also used for support ropes, called frapping cables, used on ships at sea. We find the best example using this word in the book of Acts:

> *Running under the lee*
> *of a small island called Cauda,*
> *we managed with difficulty*
> *to secure the ship's boat.*
> *After hoisting it up,*
> *they used supports [boetheia]*
> *to undergird the ship.*
> Acts 27:16-17; ESV

In this chapter, Paul was sailing to Rome as a prisoner to stand trial when the ship encountered a storm. In ancient times, ships were built entirely of wood and tar. They "...were frapped by wrapping strong ropes (4-5" diameter) or cables around the hull of the ship four or five times. During violent storms and high seas, frapping would secure the hull."[6] Frapping cables undergirded the ship in an effort to hold its planks of wood together. Without them, the ship broke apart and sailors drowned.

These words and Scripture in which we find them give us a more accurate and vibrant picture of the role God created woman to play in His story. Though women – and men – may start as unskilled apprentices, the Creator equips them to become helpers as He is a helper of His people. He calls them to be protectors and strong rescuers who bring critical aid in urgent situations. God created women to be "frapping cables" that undergird and hold together the "community ships" of society when we encounter life's storms.

THE FRAPPING CABLES OF ADVENT

If we trace the role and position of *ezer* from the first woman, Eve, we can easily diminish her meaning to fit the traditional and cultural views of women at the time and to the definition we mentioned earlier from the dictionary. The patriarchal society of ancient Israel circumscribed the role of women as centered on their families. Women were often perceived as too small to count. They had no vote, could not inherit, and were more often than not portrayed as the weaker of the two sexes.

Some women today still struggle with feeling too small to count. Recently I visited a community service organization where I met several women who overcame great obstacles – divorce, job loss, homelessness, poverty, and sexual or physical abuse – to shift their circumstances from languishing to thriving. Every one of their stories began with some version of "I thought I was too small to count."

Likewise, if we skim the Bible through the lens of ancient Israel's culture and Webster's definition of helper, we miss the number of women mentioned who fulfilled God's intended image of a helper. Three of those women are the women of Advent – Mary, Elizabeth, and Anna.

When asked to speak at a Christmas dinner for our church, the Spirit immediately pressed upon my heart to speak of these three women and the legacy they left for all women. I started my presentation by polling the audience's level of awareness about the women of Advent. Everyone knew Mary, the mother of Jesus. About half the audience was familiar with Elizabeth, the mother of John the Baptist. Only two or three knew the third and final woman, Anna.

These three generations of women were the frapping cables of Advent. They were the helpers who stood beside the men – Joseph, Zechariah, and Simeon – with the needed voice and assistance that undergirded a critical moment in the story of Christ's birth. They played a supporting role, as we all do, in God's blockbuster movie about His restoring the world and relationships with humankind. Yet, their strength of character held the story together. Their trust in and obedience to God's Word ensured that history moved forward as God intended in the face of disaster, disappointment, and dissent.

My hope in writing this study is to empower and encourage women to live into the helper image for which God created us. Using as examples the roles Mary, Elizabeth, and Anna played within the Christmas narrative, we will:

1. Explore each woman's story and legacy of what it means to be an *ezer-* or *boetheia*-styled woman;

2. Pause to reflect on how each of these women's lives and lessons applies and still speaks through the ages to women today; and finally,

3. Consider how to respond personally and intentionally to their legacy by fulfilling the potential God put in each of us as His *ezers,* wherever and within whatever circumstances we find ourselves.

REFLECT|

Take a moment and reflect on these questions. What does the Scriptural use of the word *helper* say to you...

- About God?

- About women?

- About the relationship between God and women?

CONNECT THE DOTS AND MAKE IT PERSONAL|

- Where do you fall on the continuum defining the role of a helper? Do you lean more towards seeing yourself as "too small to count" or seeing yourself as "frapping cables that undergird and hold together the ship? (Note: Your "ship" might be your family, workplace, community, or some other group.) Or do you fall somewhere in between?

- Read Psalm 10:14; 30:10-11; 54:4; and 72:12-14 and Hebrews 13:6. How do these verses and your understanding of the Greek and Hebrew definitions of *helper* alter how you think about yourself as a helper in God's unfolding story?

➢ How is God transforming the affections of your heart about being a helper?

➢ What is God calling you to do differently today to live into being a *boetheia*-helper with humankind?

The Three Women of Advent

ELIZABETH
LUKE 1:5-80

HER LIFE STORY|

The story of Advent begins with Elizabeth and her husband Zechariah. Found only in the opening chapter of the gospel of Luke, we see God at work in a most unexpected way.

Zechariah served in the temple as a priest, from the order of Abijah. His wife Elizabeth was a descendant of Aaron, the brother of Moses and the first high priest of the Hebrew nation. They lived in Judea near Jerusalem.

Luke referred to both Elizabeth and Zechariah as *"...righteous before God, living blamelessly according to all the commandments and regulations of the Lord"* (Luke 1:6, NRSV). Her name means "God is my oath,"[7] meaning "He is my good fortune or my fullness." Yet, Elizabeth was not living up to her name. She bore the misfortune of being barren, without children.

In Biblical times, the role and responsibility of women was to provide their husbands with children, especially a son. The source of this primary duty was attached to the Abrahamic

Covenant. It called the Hebrew people to be fruitful (to reproduce). Failure to procreate was a failure to live up to that covenant and brought great public shame.[8]

The patriarchal society of the Old Testament stories looked upon barrenness as a curse or punishment from God (see Genesis 16:2; 20:18; 1 Samuel 1:5-7). Though Elizabeth appeared to live a righteous life, she would have borne looks of doubt or judgment from other men and women, wondering what unseen, unconfessed sin would lead God to punish her thusly.

Then, late in life and beyond her child-bearing days, Elizabeth's long years of praying, waiting, and hoping ended. God was about to fulfill her unfulfilled dream to bear a child. While performing his duties at the temple, an angel appeared to Zechariah. The angel announced that their dream was about to come true. Elizabeth would give birth, and the name of her dream was to be John.

Imagine Elizabeth's surprise as the impossible became possible. The unexpected now expected. Imagine the deep, abiding joy she must have experienced as months passed and the child grew inside her aged, once infertile womb. Read aloud and hear her words as Elizabeth proclaimed,

> *This is what the Lord has done for me*
> *when he looked favorably on me and*
> *took away the disgrace I have endured*
> *among my people.*
> Luke 1:25; NRSV

During the third trimester of Elizabeth's pregnancy, her relative[9] Mary visited. As soon as Elizabeth heard Mary's greeting, the child in her womb leaped for joy. Elizabeth was filled with the Holy Spirit and discerned that Mary, too, carried a child, the Son of God.[10]

By this time in her pregnancy, Elizabeth surely felt the usual movements of her baby. As she went about her daily chores, she sensed the kicks and turns of John in her expanding womb. When laying in her bed at night she may have even seen his foot or fist protrude against her stomach wall.

Yet, this leap at Mary's arrival was different. This flutter of John, who grew inside Elizabeth, differed from previous sensations of her baby boy's presence. Through the power of the Holy Spirit that filled her, Elizabeth recognized Mary's voice as the voice of God, revealing to Elizabeth that she was in the presence of the mother of her Lord.

Luke tells us that Mary remained with Elizabeth for about three months before she returned home. What whispers of wonder must these two women have exchanged with each other? Mary is in the first trimester of an astonishing pregnancy by the Holy Spirit. Elizabeth in the last trimester of an equally surprising pregnancy in her advanced years. We don't know if Mary was present at John's birth, but we can imagine what joy must have filled their hearts as they supported each other and prepared for the birth of their miracle babies.

At last, the day arrived for Elizabeth. She bore a son. Her neighbors and relatives came to rejoice with her.

On the eighth day, a decisive moment for Elizabeth and Zechariah also arrived; a crossroads in which they would choose obedience or disobedience to God who had shown them great mercy. Luke tells their story, saying:

On the eighth day they came
to circumcise the child,
and they were going to name him
Zechariah after his father.
But his mother said,
"No, he is to be called John."
They said to her,
"None of your relatives has this name."
And they began motioning
to his father to find out
what name he wanted to give him.
He [Zechariah, who the angel
had made mute for doubting]
asked for a writing tablet and wrote,
"His name is John."
And all of them were amazed.
Luke 1:59-63; NRSV

According to tradition, Elizabeth's relatives and neighbors pushed her to name her child "Junior," or at least to give him a name already found on the family tree. Instead, she and Zechariah responded with obedience to the favor God showed them through the birth of this son in their advanced years. They called the child of their dream John, whose name means "The Lord is gracious and merciful." This boy became John the Baptist, who prepared the way for the Messiah Jesus to save his people through the sacrifice of the cross.

At last, Elizabeth lived into her name. As her story unfolded, she both mirrored and substantiated what it means to declare, "In God is my oath, my good fortune."

HER LEGACY AND LESSONS

Elizabeth leaves us a legacy of the importance of affirmation – affirmation of the goodness of God as well as affirming the goodness He puts in others.

AFFIRM GOD'S GOODNESS

Elizabeth's inability to bear a child left her vulnerable to judgment and pity within her community. Through her years of waiting and praying, she faced a choice – how to respond. She could live in bitterness, despair, and disillusionment with God, or she could walk in faith that her Lord had not abandoned her.

Despite what seemed a dashed hope, Elizabeth continued to affirm the goodness of God. She lived a righteous life. In fact, before introducing her story, Luke takes great pains to tell us that she and Zechariah were *"...living blamelessly according to all the commandments and regulations of the Lord"* (Luke 1:6, NRSV).

Following God's commandments can lead to expectation of His favor upon our lives; expectation that He will fulfill our heartfelt dreams. We can only imagine how Elizabeth must have experienced frustration and deep disappointment in her unfulfilled desire for a child. Yet, although all her efforts and right living did not yield her hoped-for results, she never let go of God. Instead, she lived in the tension between both her dream and her belief in God as a God of hope.

By living out her days "blamelessly according to all the commandments," Elizabeth affirmed her faith in the Lord and His goodness. Her faith did not depend on the outcome of her wants and wishes but on who she knew God to be. Elizabeth held fast to her relationship with God as her Rock, her Fortress, her Deliverer, her Refuge, her Shield, her Salvation, and her Stronghold.[11] She trusted in His goodness and remained His faithful servant.

This is the kind of faith and relationship with God that we, too, must pursue in the face of pain, suffering, and disappointment. As columnist Michael Gerson so adeptly described it, we must understand that our God of hope is the One "…who offers a different kind of security [hope] than the fulfillment of our deepest wishes. He promises a transformation of the heart in which we release the burden of our desires, and live in expectation of God's unfolding purposes, until all his mercies stand revealed."[12]

Elizabeth, trusting God's goodness, reminds us, too, that unanswered prayer does not always mean "no." Sometimes it does. Yet, at other times, silence means only that God is in the process of answering our prayer. He is working on our heart's desire to come about in His way and at His pace.

We may rest assured that in the fullness of God's timing, when all things are in place, He will conceive in us that God-given dream or hope…perhaps even one we never imagined. As He did with Elizabeth, He will give it a specific name, and the dream will grow in us. When that happens, affirm His goodness. Never let anyone or anything rename – or reframe –

that dream, our "John." Never let anyone or anything squelch our joy in knowing the *Lord is gracious and merciful.*

AFFIRM THE GOODNESS GOD PUTS IN OTHERS

Besides affirming God's goodness to her, Elizabeth also affirmed His goodness in Mary. Her immediate response to Mary's visit models for us a second and equally important character trait of an *ezer*-woman, that of an encourager.

Elizabeth was six months into her pregnancy when Mary came to visit. One could hardly fault Elizabeth had she been so focused and eager to share her own miracle that she missed the Holy Spirit speaking to her through John's leap in her womb. Yet, she didn't miss it.

For the four hundred years between the Old and New Testaments, the Lord remained silent. The Jewish community had only the last prophet Malachi and his last words to reverberate hope in their hearts. No other prophets rose to speak for God. As the Israelites languished in exile and oppression, no one came forward to remind them that the Lord had not forgotten His people.

Elizabeth, like all the Hebrew nation, longed and watched for the promised Savior. While she waited, Elizabeth remained attuned to God's Presence. So much so that when Mary and the Son of God arrived at Elizabeth's home, she recognized him. And she called it out.

Both Elizabeth's life and interaction with Mary are beautiful examples of what it means to look at others and to see them through the eyes of God. Not to see their flaws, weaknesses, or failures. But, to see the goodness and potential

God puts in them, to affirm it and call it out. We need to call attention to it, even though such acknowledgement and encouragement may mean that the individual surpasses00 us in greatness.

Attuned to the Holy Spirit, Elizabeth recognized and called out Mary as "blessed among women" and the "mother of my Lord" (Luke 1:41-45). Think of what that acknowledgement must have meant to Mary, a young teenager still pondering the angel's telling her she would bear the Son of God. Indeed, upon hearing Elizabeth's words, Mary's spirit ignited with rejoicing, and she magnified the Lord with her praise. Elizabeth's words encouraged Mary to live into her divine calling.

I know what it meant to me when my Bible study teacher reached out one evening to ask if I would consider teaching the nine-month Disciple Bible course the coming year. His pitch closed with him calling out the spiritual gift of teaching he saw in me. I had always dreamed of being a teacher. I even held a bachelor's degree in secondary education. But a series of circumstances and experiences killed that dream.

That fall, I stepped in to lead and facilitate the first of what became innumerable Bible studies. Each one filled my spirit with joy. Fulfilling my longing began with one discerning teacher who called out and encouraged the specific helper-role God fashioned me to play in His story. One discerning teacher re-awakened that dream and set me on the path to becoming the *ezer*-woman God intended.

We all, like Elizabeth and my Bible study teacher, are called to be messengers of hope and encouragement. We are called to see others as if through the eyes of God and to confirm His calling on their lives.

REFLECT|

Take a moment to consider how alike or different you are from Elizabeth. Reflect on these questions to consider where you can grow in affirming the goodness of God and the goodness that God puts in those individuals with whom He connects you.

> ➤ What does Elizabeth's story say to you about God?

> ➤ What does Elizabeth's story say to you about women?

> ➤ What does Elizabeth's story say to you about the relationship between God and women?

CONNECT THE DOTS AND MAKE IT PERSONAL|

> ➤ In Psalm 18:2, David describes experiencing God as his Rock, Fortress, Deliverer, Refuge, Shield, Salvation, and Stronghold. Which of these words best describe how you experience God?

> ➤ What dream has life caused you to defer? Or what is your heart's desire that seems impossible at this point?

➢ What does your trust in God's faithfulness and goodness look like in seasons of deferred dreams?

➢ Describe a time when you thought the answer to your dream was "no," but your desire was eventually fulfilled. Describe what that time of waiting was like and the nature of your relationship with God?

➢ Columnist Michael Gerson stated that God is One "…who offers a different kind of security than the fulfillment of our deepest wishes. He promises a transformation of the heart in which we release the burden of our desires, and live in expectation of God's unfolding purposes, until all his mercies stand revealed." Do you agree or disagree? How is God calling you to think differently about your deepest desires? How is He transforming the affections of your heart?

➢ Who has spoken life into you, by naming and acknowledging your potential? Describe how you felt about that acknowledgement.

➢ Into whose life can you speak? And how?

> What is God calling you to do differently today to live into the legacy and lessons left by Elizabeth?

RESPOND INTENTIONALLY|

- ✓ Using a Bible dictionary, study the meaning and look up scriptures that use the word "hope" (or *elpis* in Greek). Journal how this kind of hope might alter your feelings about your dreams and deepest desires. Describe how this kind of hope would transform your relationship and faith in God.

- ✓ Pray about your heart's desire. If God has not said "no," then wait and watch for Him at work. Watch for small steps you can take now toward equipping or preparing yourself for the fulfillment of your dream.

- ✓ Share and name your heart's desire with your pastor or trusted Christian friend. Explore options of how it might be fulfilled, even in surprising ways.

- ✓ If God said "no" to your heart's desire, pray that He will transform your heart to release you from the burden of that dream. Pray that the Holy Spirit will help you to discern and live into the unfolding expectations of His purposes in your life.

- ✓ Do you see goodness and potential in someone who may not recognize that for themselves? Share with another person what goodness you see in them and why.

- ✓ What other ways can you affirm God's goodness in your life and affirm His goodness in others?

Mary

Luke 1:26-56; 2:1-52

Her Life Story |

Can you imagine being fourteen or fifteen years old and, while doing your daily chores, an angel of the Lord shows up to declare:

Greetings, favored one!
The Lord is with you...
Do not be afraid, Mary,
for you have found favor with God.
Luke 1:28, 30; NRSV

Mary came from humble means. She lived in Nazareth, a tiny village nestled in a basin overlooking the Esdraelon valley. Located in the southern most hills of the Lebanon mountain range in northern Israel, Nazareth was secluded from Israel's main trade routes. It was of so little consequence that one day Nathanael would declare, "Nazareth! Can anything good come from there?" when beckoned to come and see the long-awaited Messiah (John 1:46).

The insignificance of her hometown coupled with Mary growing up in a strong patriarchal society likely left her with the impression that she was too small to count. Yet, Mary was not too small to count in God's eyes. In fact, she was so favored that the Lord sent His angel, Gabriel, to announce that she would bear the Son of God.

The Greek word used for "favored" in this verse is *charitoo*, from the word *charis*,[13] defined as *grace or kindness*. Scripture uses this term to describe the Lord's disposition to extend Himself, to lean and reach toward people to bless them.[14] For the Lord to favor someone is for Him to extend His grace to them in a way that blesses them.

The dictionary defines the verb "favor" as "to choose or select." A more dated and informal use of the word indicates when someone resembles or looks like someone or something else. For instance, for a child to favor a parent or relative, means they look like, bear resemblance to, or remind us of their mother or father.

So, what does the angel's greeting as "favored one" tell us about Mary? It lets us know up front that Mary's character traits must resemble those of the Lord. They remind us of our Father and Creator. Mary's demeanor, attitude, and goodness must have been those that made God smile.[15] So, He leaned toward this woman-child made in His image and extended to her an unimaginable blessing. He chose her to bear His One and Only Son. He picked her as the mother to birth, nurture, and raise the Messiah who would save the world.

Since she was a virgin, Mary asked how she could be the mother of the Messiah. The angel said that she would conceive through the Holy Spirit of God, for whom nothing is impossible. Mary responded to the angel's pronouncement simply and humbly, saying:

> *"Behold the maidservant of the Lord!*
> *Let it be to me according to your word."*
> Luke 1:38; NRSV

She never balked or bargained. She simply accepted. Her response is remarkable given that she must have known the possible implications under Jewish law. Mary was engaged to Joseph. What would appear as having an intimate relationship outside of marriage meant she could be ostracized by her community, turned out of her family home, or even stoned to death (see Deuteronomy 22:13-21).

Joseph could call off the wedding, and Mary would live in shame. We don't know if these consequences raced through Mary's mind at the moment, but we do know her answer to the angel's words. She simply received the gift of God's grace.

We do, however, get a glimpse into Mary's heart in the verses that follow. She hastily packed her bags and traveled to the home of her relative Elizabeth and Zachariah. Upon entering, Elizabeth immediately recognized and called out Mary as blessed and "the mother of my Lord" (Luke 1:43). Rather than wailing or bemoaning her predicament, Mary responded with a song of praise to the Lord. Her Magnificat exalts God for His mercy and blessings. She magnified His name. Mary bore witness to His faithfulness and love for His people, singing:

> *My soul glorifies the Lord and*
> *my spirit rejoices in God my Savior,*
> *for he has been mindful of the*
> *humble state of his servant.*
> *From now on all generations*
> *will call me blessed,*
> *for the Mighty One has done great things*
> *for me— holy is his name.*
> *His mercy extends to those who fear him,*
> *from generation to generation.*
> *He has performed mighty deeds*
> *with his arm;*
> *he has scattered those who are proud*
> *in their inmost thoughts.*
> *He has brought down rulers*
> *from their thrones*
> *but has lifted up the humble.*
> *He has filled the hungry with good things*
> *but has sent the rich away empty.*
> *He has helped his servant*
> *Israel, remembering to be merciful*
> *to Abraham and his descendants forever, just*
> *as he promised our ancestors.*
> Luke 1:47-55, NIV

HER LEGACY AND LESSONS |

As the mother of Jesus, Mary left us a rich legacy of what it looks like to yield to God's call upon our lives, to display a nurturing spirit, and to magnify the Lord.

YIELD AND TRUST IN GOD

Before moving forward with a risky or life altering change, our more natural inclination is to conduct a cost/benefit analysis. We draw a line down the middle of a page. We list advantages on the left and disadvantages on the right. We weigh potential gains and losses, possible plusses and minuses. Then we decide. Do we move forward or not? If yes, how?

Scripture tells us that Mary pondered the angel's pronouncement in her heart (Luke 2:29). Perhaps she wondered why she, of all Jewish women, was chosen? What would her future be? What divine purpose would her Son fulfill?

Yet, the one thing Mary never questioned was whether she would accept or decline the pronouncement and its implications. She never argued or whined about possible ostracism, the possible disowning by family and fiancé, or worse yet, being stoned to death.

Mary taught us what it means to yield and trust in God. Her ponderings may have included a cost/benefit analysis. Yet, its purpose would have been to know and prepare her heart for what may happen as a result. Its purpose was not to decide *IF* she would yield. Yielding was never in question.

*Mary's hope was not in an outcome.
Her hope was in the Lord.*

The Greek word for *hope*, *elpis*, translates as the expectation of something good — not the "trying to think positively so something good might happen" type of hope, but the "expectation it actually will occur." This expectation comes not from personal effort or power, but from the expectation and trust in God's promise of unconditional love for those who both believe in Him and believe Him.

This *elpis*-like hope inspired and enabled Mary to yield without question, to press forward despite the brewing storm of possible pain and suffering that awaited her. Like Mary, if the frapping cables of trust in God's goodness encircle us, we can yield and weather difficulties or challenges we encounter. Though we cannot see the future, we can live totally dependent on Him for protection and provision.

Nurture Faith in the Lord

To nurture is to take care of another such that they grow, develop, or succeed. It is about enabling. God assigned Mary, this young, too-small-to-count woman, the responsibility of caring for and nurturing His Son, the Savior of the world. What a tremendous accountability this role carried.

Jewish women's lives centered on their families. In his article about the woman's role in Judaism, Rabbinic scholar and author, Rabbi Nissan Dovid Dubov, described a Jewish wife and mother. He wrote,[16]

> *...the very Jewishness of a person is dependent on the mother...In a Jewish household, the wife and mother is called in Hebrew akeret habayit. This means literally the "mainstay" of the home. It is she who largely determines the character and atmosphere of the entire home... It is a home where God's Presence is felt every day of the week; and not only when engaged in prayer and learning Torah but also when engaged in very ordinary activities such as eating and drinking etc., in accordance with the directive, "Know Him in all your ways."*

As a mother, Mary was the one not only to show Jesus great love but also to instill within him godly virtues. She was the mainstay, tasked with passing on the Scriptures and Jewish traditions of faith. Given the Hebrew mother's role, we might surmise that Jesus first heard the prophecies of the Old Testament from Mary. Perhaps through her retelling of Gabriel's visit with her, Jesus discovered He was the fulfillment of those prophecies.

Perhaps, too, as Jesus listened to his birth story, he repeatedly heard his mother's simple response, *"Let it be to me according to your word"* (Luke 1:38, NRSV). I wonder if those words came to his mind the night he knelt to pray in the Garden of Gethsemane, wrestling with the brutal suffering that was to come. Did his mother's words and life play a role in empowering Jesus to declare likewise as she did, *'Father,...not my will but yours be done"* (Luke 22:42b, NRSV)? Did her faith and lessons help strengthen him to surrender willingly to the soldiers that night and to do so with such power and calm authority that *"...they stepped back and fell to the ground"* (John 18:6, NRSV).

Mary left us a legacy of what it means to nurture another. Whether we have biological children or not, God created women to be *ezer*-helpers for all. He created us to serve Him as the *boetheia*, or supporting cables, who wrap His unconditional love and care around all creation, to rescue them from the discouragement of pain, suffering, and loss.

We are God's mainstay, whose responsibility is to impress upon children and grandchildren the Word of God. He calls us to school others in the traditions of our faith, instill godly virtues, and open them to the divine destinies God has placed upon their lives. We are to ensure that all generations that come after us will know God and all His ways.

Exalt and Magnify the Lord

A microscope takes the smallest thing and enlarges it such that details once hidden become visible and evident to the naked eye. It does not change the actual size of the object viewed but magnifies it.

Mary's song of praise did just that with God. She magnified His greatness and goodness. She bore witness to a detail others may have missed – namely His concern for the lowly, insignificant, and disadvantaged. She connected the dots from the mighty acts experienced to their true source – not human effort, but God at work. As Mary poured out her soul in praise, she lifted up God as the Savior and Provider for all generations. What others might overlook or dismiss, Mary exalted.

We will never enlarge God to be greater than He already is. However, we can help enlarge the lens through which others see Him. We do so when we, like Mary, bear witness to His power, provision, and faithfulness; when we attribute God with the impossible made possible; when we sing praises to His mighty acts of love within, through, and for us. We can sing out loud to ensure everyone sees clearly and specifically the root source of our help:

> *My help comes from the Lord,*
> *the Maker of heaven and earth.*
> *He will not let your foot slip—*
> *he who watches over you will not slumber;*
> *indeed, he who watches over Israel*
> *will neither slumber nor sleep.*
> Psalm 121:2-4, NIV

REFLECT|

Take a moment to consider how alike or different you are from Mary.

- ➤ What does Mary's story say to you about God?

- ➤ What does Mary's story say to you about women?

- ➤ What does Mary's story say to you about the relationship between God and women?

CONNECT THE DOTS AND MAKE IT PERSONAL|

- ➢ Where is God calling you to yield even though there may be a cost? What holds you back from stepping forward.

- ➢ How is God calling you to think differently about *hope?*

- ➢ Who and how are you called to *nurture*, serving as the supporting cables of God's love with others; schooling them in the traditions of our faith; acting as role models of godly virtues; and encouraging others into God's calling on their life?

- ➢ How can you exalt or magnify the Lord and His goodness in your life?

- ➢ What is God calling you to do differently today to live into the legacy and lessons left by Mary?

RESPOND INTENTIONALLY |

- ✓ If you identified where God is calling you to yield, make the commitment to step forward without reservations. Pray as Mary prayed, *"Behold the maidservant of the Lord! Let it be to me according to your word."* Then go ahead and identify the possible costs. Plan how you can proceed or move through them if they do occur.

- ✓ Identify ways you can pass on the Scriptures and traditions of your faith.
   - Volunteer to teach a Sunday school class.
   - Get involved in a youth program or ministry.
   - Participate in a small group study.
   - Commit to heart verses that are most meaningful to you; share them with others to encourage them in whatever situation they may face.
   - Attend a class or read a book about how best to share the difference Christ has made in your life, so that you are ready to do so when the opportunity arises.
   - Share your story with a child or grandchild.

- ✓ Think about the favor God has poured out on you. Put Mary's Magnificat in your own words and experiences. Write a prayer-song of praise and thanks for what He has done or is doing in and around you.

- ✓ The personal stories in my devotional, *Connecting the Dots: Learning to Live a Word-Shaped Life* put the work of the Lord in my life under the "microscope." Write a short devotional or story that exalts the Lord and His work in your life. Magnify Him by sharing your story with another individual.

- ✓ Bear witness to God's faithfulness and compassion. Share your devotional or story with someone who is struggling. Share it with someone for whom your heart breaks as they stumble without Jesus.

ANNA

LUKE 2:22-38

HER LIFE STORY |

Only a handful of women may remember her. Yet, Luke gives value and voice to Anna in his gospel by naming her heritage and calling out her gift as a prophet. In Luke 2:36-38 we learn several facts about Anna:

—She was the daughter of Phaneul from the tribe of Asher, who was the eighth son of Jacob and the second by Leah's maidservant Zilpah (Genesis 30:13).

—Like most Hebrew women, she married at an early age (at 14 or 15 years.)

—Her husband died after only seven years of marriage. His death left Anna a widow, a difficult status in ancient times as her livelihood and survival depended on her husband.

—At the time Luke introduces us to Anna, she lived as an 84-year-old widow and prophet. She was one of only a handful of women in Scripture who spoke for God and communicated His message.

Anna's life unraveled at the devastating loss of her husband. Her vision of how she might flourish as a wife and mother in a Hebrew culture dimmed. She retreated to the only safe haven she knew – the temple. There, she devoted herself to her divine calling.

Luke tells us, "She never left the temple" (Luke 2:37). Some scholars interpret that to mean she resided in the courts of the temple. Others believe it means only that she was a frequent or constant presence both day and night, coming to worship, pray, and fast.

Whatever her residential status, she came to patiently wait and watch. Anna knew the words of Old Testament prophets about a coming Messiah. As a prophet herself, she would claim and proclaim that promise. Despite her personal circumstances, Anna never lost hope, biblically defined as the confident assurance God was with her and the Savior would one day come as promised.

Because of her faithfulness, Anna was at the temple when Mary and Joseph brought Jesus eight days after his birth, to be circumcised according to Jewish tradition. Simeon, who God promised would not die before seeing the Messiah appear, was also there. Simeon recognized the baby and publicly announced Jesus' divine destiny.

Scripture does not say exactly what caught Anna's attention that day. She may have stood nearby when Simeon spoke the baby's identity. She may have wandered over to the crowd that gathered around Simeon and the parents, or the Holy Spirit quickened her spirit to recognize the promised Messiah.

Whatever it was at that moment, God rewarded Anna for her faithful devotion and never-wavering in hope. He gave her the gift of seeing the Messiah-child. For that, she gave thanks. And then, so great was her gratitude and joy that she could not stop talking about him.

HER LEGACY AND LESSONS|

Although Anna is mentioned in only three short verses throughout Scripture, her story packs a powerful spiritual legacy for us today. Anna left us with two.

HOW TO WAIT

Anna first showed us how best to wait upon the Lord – faithfully and expectantly, never surrendering our hope and peace. We can wait in confident hope that God will indeed deliver us. We can wait in peace despite circumstances because we can trust in His faithfulness and promises.

Waiting faithfully and expectantly does not imply that we wait passively. Instead, we are busy staying in the Word and serving as God's image-bearers. At the time of Anna's story, she had aged in place and resided in what I lovingly call life's Act 3. Others know it as the senior years, the third third of life, our finishing season. Even so, she remained actively involved in serving the Lord.

Anna continued to flourish despite losses and challenges. Neither age nor circumstances deterred her from standing strong as His *boetheia*-prophet in the temple. She never "retired" as we think about vocational retirement today. Her life was not centered on hobbies or relaxing by the pool with her favorite drink on a hot desert-like day. Even in her advanced years, Anna served God while keeping an eye out for the Messiah.

As I myself aged into Act 3, I noticed my pace slowed, my energy level weakened faster, and the quantity of productive output lessened. However, my love of sitting with God and His Word increased. My focus sharpened to the meaningful few places I felt called to serve. My productivity, or fruitfulness, remained steady and sweeter because I could draw upon years of experiences and hard-gained wisdom now in my toolbox.

I have discovered that there is no such thing as "lay-offs" in God's kingdom here on earth. Even in dry, desert days, God opens to us opportunities to flourish. Even in the last third of life, God still employs us and works through us.

Eighty-seven-year-old Erin Lail shared best how God looks at our aging process. She remembered her aged grandmother writing to her, "Though there be but few strings left on the harp of life, God can still play upon it a 'Hallelujah Chorus.'" Ms. Lail continued, "I'm not at all accustomed to old age, though I'm making friends with it. Isn't God merciful that old age is a gradual process?"[17] Amen to that!

We all age through seasons of life. Everyone experiences different physical, mental, social, and personal ups and downs. Yet, wherever and however old we are, one constant remains. We can continue to grow and serve our Lord. We can continue to thrive and blossom in the most desert-like conditions.

As the prophet Isaiah succinctly put it, and Anna's life so aptly modeled,

> *"The wilderness and the dry land*
> *shall be glad,*
> *the desert shall rejoice and blossom;*
> *like the crocus it shall blossom abundantly,*
> *and rejoice with joy and singing."*
> Isaiah 35:1; NRSV

As we journey to the manger and look forward to Christ's second coming, we, too, must remain watchful. In the meantime, we must continue to grow through His Word. We must never cease to make ourselves available to His call and assignments as we wait to see Christ face-to-face.

Never Stop Talking About Him

Secondly, while Anna bore witness to the prophecies of a coming Messiah, once she found him, she never stopped talking about him.

Pastor-teacher John MacArthur best described Anna's legacy of witness when he wrote,

> *She continually spoke of Him to all*
> *who were looking for the Redeemer.*
> *This became her one message for the*
> *rest of her life."*[18]

Anna would know (because of her role at the temple) who the believing remnant were. She could identify the true worshipers – the ones who, like her, were expectantly awaiting the Messiah. She sought such people out, and at every opportunity from then on, she spoke to them about Him. Anna thus became one of the very first and most enduring witnesses of Christ.

The Redeemer had come. Anna knew that the ancient prophets' words would now be fulfilled. The long-awaited and hoped-for salvation and redemption arrived with this baby. Knowing this, we, like Anna, must bear continual witness to who He is as the promised Son of God, Savior, and Lord of Lords. He is the one message for the rest of our life on earth.

Jesus commissioned all Christians with the agency and authority to spread the good news to all nations and peoples.[19] Our sharing who Christ is and what He has done for us prepares the way for others to experience His redemptive work as well. Sharing our stories and the difference Christ has made in our life clears the path for possibility – that is, hope. Opening up about our experiences infuses others with hope that what He did for us, He will do for them as well. It reassures another that the power and presence of God in our life is available to them, too.

When we live into waiting expectantly and faithfully, we want to move forward, never to stop beckoning others as the apostle Andrew did, saying,

"Come, we have found the Messiah"
John 1:41; NRSV.

REFLECT|

Anna's legacy leaves us with provocative questions to ponder:

- ➢ What does Anna's story say to you about God?

- ➢ What does Anna's story say to you about women?

- ➢ What does Anna's story say to you about the relationship between God and women?

CONNECT THE DOTS AND MAKE IT PERSONAL|

- ➢ Where are you waiting, perhaps a long time, to realize the fulfillment of God's promises?

- ➢ What word(s) best describes how you are waiting?
    - o Expectantly
    - o With Hope and Peace
    - o Anxiously
    - o Confused
    - o Distractedly

- o Self-Absorbed
- o Centered on Serving
- o Other?

➤ How might God be calling you to think differently about the waiting seasons of life?

➤ What spiritual disciplines does the Scripture imply Anna used to strengthen her ability to wait for the Lord?

➤ Consider the spiritual disciplines of quiet time in prayer, meditation, fasting, study, simplicity, solitude, service, or worship. Which one(s) do you practice regularly? Which one(s) might you practice more intentionally that better enable you to wait faithfully on the Lord? To be an enduring witness for Christ?

➤ Like Anna, while you wait and watch for His return, are you being an enduring witness for Jesus Christ? If no, what holds you back from sharing your relationship with Christ with others? If yes, how and where can you share most effectively? With whom might Christ be leading you to share?

➢ What is God calling you to do differently today to live into the legacy and lessons left by Anna?

RESPOND INTENTIONALLY|

✓ Expect Christ to show up each day. Let the first words of your morning be "Come, Lord. Reveal yourself to me this day."

✓ Practice the Daily Examen. At the end of each day, review what happened to determine:
  o where you met Christ.
  o Or where you missed him.
  o At what moment did you feel the closest to Christ? Or the most distant?

✓ Write or journal a prayer of thanksgiving for where Christ meets you during your day.

✓ What spiritual discipline or habit can you engage in that moves you back toward God, living in a more Christ-like way, and watching more intentionally for His Presence?

- ✓ Write or journal your story of the difference commitment and following Jesus Christ as Savior and Lord have made in your life. Practice and be ready to share that story when the opportunity arises. As with Anna,

> *... at that very hour she began*
> *to give thanks to God*
> *and to speak of him to all who were waiting*
> *for the redemption of Jerusalem.*
> Luke 2:38; ESV

A Closing Note

A pastor talked about a time when he prepared for his Sunday sermon. His little daughter came in and said, "Daddy, can we play?"

He answered, "I'm awfully sorry, sweetheart, but I'm right in the middle of preparing this sermon. In about an hour, I can play."

She said, "Okay, when you're finished, Daddy, I'm going to give you a great big hug."

He thanked her, and she went to the door. There she did a U-turn and came back to give her father what he described as "a chiropractic, bone-breaking hug."

The pastor looked at his daughter quizzically and said, "Darling, I thought you said you were going to give me a hug *after* I finished."

His daughter answered without missing a beat, "Daddy, I just wanted you to know what you have to look forward to!"[20]

The Three Women of Advent

Advent reminds us of what God wants us to know. The first coming of His Son, Jesus, is only a foreshadowing of what we have to look forward to in His great second coming.

In the meantime, the three women of Advent leave us with a legacy of how to live while we wait and watch expectantly with believer's hope. In doing so, Mary, Elizabeth, and Anna served as models of what God created women to be – helpers through whom He gave the needed strength, power, protection, and support for the moment. They rescued and moved the story of Christ's birth forward toward His ultimate victory over death and our redemption. Mary, Elizabeth, and Anna remind us: No woman-helper is too small to count.

The lives of these three women teach us how best to wait and watch expectantly. With a believer's hope, we yield completely, love and nurture unconditionally. We name and hold onto our dreams and magnify the Lord, giving Him all the credit. We affirm God's goodness and faithfulness, and thus inspire others to live into that same hope. We continue to grow and serve our Lord, whenever and however He calls us, moving from one strength to another as we wait to be reunited with our Lord.

As the psalmist proclaimed,

> *As they go through the Valley of Baca,*
> *They make it a place of springs;*
> *The early rain also covers it with pools.*
> *They go from strength to strength;*
> *The God of gods will be seen in Zion.*
> Psalm 84:6-7, NRSV

Let me share one last story I heard over dinner with friends one evening. It serves as a closing metaphor for what it means when we live as *ezer* or *boetheia*-styled women.

The bottle of Chanel perfume promised intoxicating fragrance when it left France during World War II. An American soldier struck a bargain with one of the few manufacturers whose building still stood after the Paris bombings. To supplement his army pay, he bought and sold bottles of the perfume to his buddies for their sweethearts and family. One bottle traveled across the ocean to his mother who waited for him back home.

After telling that story, our dinner host, the soldier's brother, retrieved the now 70-year-old perfume from the bedroom. The vintage cologne had turned dark amber, the color of aged whiskey. Time and disuse fused its dauber to the top of the softly curved glass bottle. The fragrance forever trapped inside, possibly deteriorated, and foul smelling.

In his second letter to the Corinthians, the apostle Paul likened those who spread the knowledge of Christ to spreading a fragrance (2 Corinthians 2:14-15), a bouquet of scents that promised to bless the lives of others. Both their words and actions spread the enticing sweet aroma of victory in who they were and whose they were.

Paul's imagery referenced a Roman tradition for recognizing military triumph. When a successful general marched his army through the city streets, Roman citizens positioned along the parade route signaled the general's victory by burning sweet spices. All who caught wind of the aroma knew the general returned victorious from battle.

God intended our lives to signal Christ's triumph over death by spreading the good news of His love and promise of eternal life. If we resist or refuse to live into our created nature as *ezer* and *boetheia* women, we become like that 70-year-old perfume. Over time, our hearts harden, trapping our potential inside. Our color darkens with self-centeredness. Our fragrance spoils and is forever lost on a hurting world.

***

Now, here we are, at the end of our study together. I hope you gained new insight as you re-visited the Genesis story of God's purpose in creating women. I pray that the stories of Mary, Elizabeth, and Anna offered you new perspectives about the character of the "helper" women who played such significant roles in undergirding the story of Advent. We must never allow the smallness of their part in the biblical story – nor ours in this life – detract from their significance and importance to the bigger story of God's redemption.

To sustain the new shoots of spiritual growth emerging from our time together, consider what God is saying to *you*. Reflect on your journey through this study:

—How is God empowering you to think differently about your place or legacy as a woman in your family, your church, and in your community?

—How is God re-ordering and transforming the affections of your heart?

—What are one or two things God is calling you to do or do differently as you go about your day?

I leave you with one final caveat that each of the three women of Advent discovered in living this kind of life: Our faith trusts in a Person, not an outcome. We cannot presume that who we are today is who God wants or will empower us to be in the future. Nor can we presume that everything that got us to where we are today can take us to where Jesus is now leading. Wherever He leads us, our faith in God, His character, and His ways is what will undergird us – and in turn enable us to undergird others – as we move forward, as we transform into the person He meant us to be.

So, as one year draws to an end, bless it, and then close that chapter. Get ready because, as Mary, Elizabeth, and Anna discovered, God is doing a new thing. We need only to surrender with the words of Mary,

---

*"Behold your servants, Lord.
Let it be with us according to your word."*

BECAUSE THE BEST IS YET TO COME.

NOTES

IF IT WERE NOT FOR WOMEN...

[1] Accessed online December 29, 2021, at https://www.famousinventors.org/12-famous-women-inventors-of-all-time. Several sites exist listing women who changed life as we know it because of their contributions to society.

[2] Accessed online December 29, 2021, https://www.merriam-webster.com/dictionary/helper.

[3] Accessed November 20, 2021, at https://margmowczko.com/a-suitable-helper/.

[4] I first ran across this concept in an excellent book by Susan Hunt and Barbara Thompson, *The Legacy of Biblical Womanhood*, Crossway Books, 2003, p.219.

[5] Accessed November 20, 2021 at https://biblehub.com/greek/997.htm.

[6] Accessed December 29, 2021, at complete-in-him.com/2018/03/23/my-frapping-god/

ELIZABETH|

[7] Ronald F Youngblood, general editor. "Elizabeth," *Nelson's New Illustrated Bible Dictionary*. Nashville, Tennessee: Thomas Nelson, Inc, 1995. p. 397.

[8] Torah Class, Old Testament Studies. https://www.torahclass.com/old-testament-studies-tc/38-old-testament-studies-deuteronomy/263-lesson-32-deuteronomy-23-24, Accessed 2/17/2022.

[9] The passage in Luke 1:36 uses the Greek word *suggenis*. While some versions translate that word as "cousin," others translate it as simply "relative." Elizabeth was from the tribe of Levi while Mary was from the tribe of Judah. Levi and Judah were brothers, two of the twelve sons of Israel. This would make the two women relatives and, if not first cousins, then at least distant cousins.

[10] Luke 1:41-44, NRSV.

[11] Psalm 18:2, NRSV.

[12] Michael Gerson, "Hope May Feel Elusive, But Despair is Not the Answer," *Washington Post*, December 23, 2021 (accessed online January 15, 2022).

MARY|

[13] James Strong, *The New Strong's Exhaustive Concordance of the Bible*, Nashville: Thomas Nelson Publishers, 1995. Greek #5487 and #5485.

[14] *Discovery Bible,* Accessed from BibleHub.com on 1/19/2022 at https://www.biblehub.com/greek/5485.htm.

[15] Oxford Languages – Bing Translator, accessed online 1/22/2022.

[16] Rabbi Nissan Dovid Dubov, "What is the Role of the Woman in Judaism?" Wimbledon, United Kingdom: Chabad.org. Accessed online 1/27/2022 at https://www.chabad.org/library/article_cdo/aid/1802936/jewish/Woman-in-Judaism.

ANNA

[17] Susan Hunt and Barbara Thompson, *The Legacy of Biblical Womanhood.* Wheaton, Illinois: Crossway Books, 2003. p. 181.

[18] John MacArthur, *Twelve Extraordinary Women.* Nashville, Tennessee: Thomas Nelson, Inc., 2005. p. 139.

[19] Matthew 28:18-20, NRSV.

A CLOSING NOTE

[20] Dale Bruner, "Advent, a Foreshadow of Good," PreachingToday.com. Accessed on website on 12/10/2002.

SOURCES

Shannon Bream, *The Women of the Bible Speak: The Wisdom of 16 Women and Their Lessons for Today*. Fox News Books, 2021.

Dale Bruner, "Advent, a Foreshadow of Good," *PreachingToday.com*.

Discovery Bible, BibleHub.com.

Rabbi Nissan Dovid Dubov, "What is the Role of the Woman in Judaism?" Wimbledon, United Kingdom: Chabad.org.

Michael Gerson, "Hope May Feel Elusive, But Despair is Not the Answer," *Washington Post*. December 23, 2021.

Susan Hunt and Barbara Thompson, *The Legacy of Biblical Womanhood*. Wheaton, Illinois: Crossway Books, 2003.

Rhonda Harrington Kelley, *Life Lessons from Women in the Bible*. Nashville, Tennessee: Lifeway Press, 1998.

John MacArthur, *Twelve Extraordinary Women: How God Shaped Women of the Bible and What He Wants to Do with You*. Nashville, Tennessee: Thomas Nelson, Inc., 2005.

Merriam-Webster.com/dictionary.

Oxford Languages, Online Bing Translator.

Tammy Phillips, *Complete in Him,* Blog Posts at WordPress.com.

James Strong, *The New Strong's Exhaustive Concordance of the Bible*. Nashville, Tennessee: Thomas Nelson Publishers, 1995.

Ronald F Youngblood (general editor), *Nelson's New Illustrated Bible Dictionary*. Nashville, Tennessee: Thomas Nelson, Inc, 1995.

Meet the Author

Gloria Ashby is a Christ-follower in a lifetime pursuit of God and a Word-shaped life. She connects the dots for herself and others by teaching, leading Bible studies, and mentoring in both secular and faith-based settings. Her passion is sharing God's Word and encouraging others to realize their full potential as His children.

In addition to authoring numerous inspirational stories found in *Chicken Soup for the Soul* and other devotionals, Gloria is the author of *Connecting the Dots: Learning to Live a Word-Shaped Life,* and co-author of a workbook, *My Story for God's Glory: Telling What He Has Done for Me.*

Gloria holds an undergraduate degree in Religious Education and Secondary Education, and a master's degree in Social Work. She and her husband, Jim, live in Texas. When not teaching, you can find her spending leisure mornings over scripture with a cup of hot tea, reading Christian fiction or a good mystery, tending her butterfly garden, and enjoying a game of mahjongg or canasta with friends. Gloria is the proud mom of one married daughter and two precious granddaughters who keep their Gigi and Poppy hopping.

Gloria would love to hear how this book impacted or resonated with you. To connect with her, or if you would like to schedule Gloria to speak at your event, please contact her at gloriaashby.connectingdots@gmail.com.

ALSO BY GLORIA K. ASHBY:

Connecting the Dots:
Learning to Live a Word-Shaped Life

Finalist, 2021 Christian Literary Awards, Henri Award, receiving the Seal of Excellence Medallion.

How do you know that God is always at work in your life?

Gloria connects the dots between God's truths and your everyday events, activities, and relationships. She shares seventy real-life inspirational stories to help you understand the way God works through ordinary things to reassure you of His Presence, direct your path, and woo you toward growth, confidence, and abundant faith.

Each story includes a related biblical passage and helpful suggestions in how to connect the dots between our life events and God's providence.

Take the challenge! Invite God to use these stories to spur you toward recognizing His work and activity in your life, and to become the person He created you to be.

Made in the USA
Las Vegas, NV
30 November 2022